MOROCCO

Allan Havis

BROADWAY PLAY PUBLISHING INC
New York
www.broadwayplaypublishing.com
info@broadwayplaypublishing.com

First published by B P P I in July 1989 in the collection *Plays By Allan Havis*
First printing this edition: December 2011
I S B N: 978-0-88145-512-0

Book design: Marie Donovan
Page make-up: Adobe Indesign
Typeface: Palatino
Printed and bound in the U S A

ABOUT THE AUTHOR

Productions by Allan Havis at San Diego Rep, Old Globe, Vox Nova, Seattle's A C T, Long Wharf, South Coast Rep, American Repertory Theater, Hartford Stage, Virginia Stage, Berkshire Theater Festival, Philadelphia Theater Co, and Rowholt Theater-Verlag (National German Radio). Commissions include England's Chichester Festival, Sundance, San Diego Rep, Ted Danson's Anasazi Productions, South Coast Rep, Mixed Blood, C S C Rep, Malashock Dance, & Carolina Chamber Chorale. With over 15 plays in print, other publications include a novel *Albert the Astronomer*, *American Political Plays* (2001), *American Political Plays After 9/11* (2010), & *Cult Films: Taboo & Transgression*, (2008). In collaboration with composer Anthony Davis, their opera *Lilith* premiered at U C San Diego's Conrad Prebys Hall in 2009. Recipient of Guggenheim, Rockefeller, Kennedy Center/American Express, C B S, H B O, National Endowment for the Arts Awards, & San Diego Theater Critics Circle. He earned an M F A from Yale. He is provost of Thurgood Marshall College/UC San Diego and a professor of Theater.

MOROCCO was first produced in a one act version at American Repertory Theater, Cambridge MA in April 1984. The cast and creative contributor were:

KEMPLER.. Tony Shaloub
COLONEL .... Ben Halley Jr

Director .... Gerald Chapman

The world premiere of the full length version was at Virginia Stage Company, Norfolk VA in February 1985. The cast and creative contributors were:

KEMPLER... Larry Pine
COLONEL .... Ray Aranha
MRS KEMPLER ....Gordana Rashovich
WAITER... Edward Morgan

Director .... Chris Hanna

The play was subsequently produced at W P A Theater in NY NY in June and July 1988. The cast and creative contributors were:

KEMPLER..Sam Freed
COLONEL .... George Guidall
MRS KEMPLER ....Gordana Rashovich
WAITER..Anthony Ruiz

Director ....Allan Havis

PLAYWRIGHT'S NOTE

As if in a dream, MOROCCO travels an irregular path between things of certainty and doubt. The traditional notion of plot, admittedly, has fallen by the wayside. Time may be truncated or stretched in a particular subjected manner. Logic bends to one's displeasure. During moments of anxiety, reality fools us. Something may seem unreal, or far worse—hyperbolic. To inhabit a Max Ernst canvas for a day, a week, a month, would be most frightening. And yet, there is a comic afterthought to this cold clammy sweat.

An American discovers that he is in a foreign land, without clear purpose or credentials, and in growing conflict with his better instincts. He pretends that, perhaps, the next morning will be brighter. Naked, his speech is distilled and terse. He stands at a threshold.

CHARACTERS

MR.KEMPLER—*an architect in his late thirties working for a New York firm with clandestine contracts overseas. He is punctual, fastidious, and somewhat arrogant. His anger is slow to surface, although he manages to go through the motions. He is affluent, with experience in business kickbacks. He has been married for ten years and travels with his wife.*

COLONEL—*a much older man of Arab nationality. He has never seen foreign duty. Overweight and a chain smoker, he gives the appearance of an anxious man about to retire. His position is senior officer at a Moroccan jail for women. His sense of irony is broad and he cannot stifle a bad joke. He thinks his life could improve with a little luck. He deals with whores, drug dealers and thieves. He takes pride in his difficult exterior. He has yet to arrest an American in his city.*

MRS KEMPLER—*an unusually alluring woman in her mid-thirties. She is part Latin, part Arabian. Educated in England, she has only a slight Mediterranean accent. She hides very little about herself, but answers all pointed questions as though she were a day-born child. The cleverness inside her is unassuming and soft, and emerges in casual tones.*

WAITER

SETTING

Time: The present year.

Place:
ACT ONE: *Fez, Morocco*
ACT TWO: *Malaga, Spain*
ACT THREE: *Fez, Morocco*

to Ken and Ginger Baldwin for their generous,
enthusiastic supporting of new plays and exciting
original theater over so many years

ACT ONE

(Fez, Morocco. The COLONEL's *office inside the jailhouse.)*

DAY ONE

COLONEL: Is this a picture of your wife?

KEMPLER: Yes, I believe so.

COLONEL: And her wardrobe?

KEMPLER: I don't recognize it.

COLONEL: And have you seen these? *(More photos)*

KEMPLER: I don't quite understand.

COLONEL: *(Pause)* Please, have a seat.

KEMPLER: Is she here?

COLONEL: Yes. *(Offering a cigarette)*

KEMPLER: No, thanks. I don't smoke.

COLONEL: I understand you are an architect.

KEMPLER: Yes.

COLONEL: That's quite impressive. Working very hard?

KEMPLER: Yes.

COLONEL: Work is wonderful for the spirit.

KEMPLER: I'm sure.

COLONEL: It says in my report that your wife is a banker.

KEMPLER: That is correct.

COLONEL: An executive?

KEMPLER: Yes.

COLONEL: We treat bankers very well.

KEMPLER: How kind of you.

COLONEL: Do I cause you great embarrassment, Mister Kempler?

KEMPLER: Not at all.

COLONEL: Wives sometime misbehave.

KEMPLER: You must have confused her with someone else.

COLONEL: I don't believe so.

KEMPLER: Are you head of staff?

COLONEL: Colonel, yes.

KEMPLER: Perhaps you can tell me why she was apprehended.

COLONEL: Certainly. *(Pause)* Prostitution, disorderly conduct, drunkenness.

KEMPLER: That's absurd.

COLONEL: *(Amused)* Of course. *(Pause)* And you wish to post bail?

KEMPLER: Yes, naturally.

COLONEL: I think we can arrange something. *(Pause)* Your wife spent last night sleepless.

KEMPLER: Is she all right?

COLONEL: Reasonable well.

KEMPLER: When may I see her?

COLONEL: Shortly. She's now with our medics.

KEMPLER: She was kept in a cell last night?

COLONEL: Yes.

KEMPLER: Why wasn't I phoned earlier?

COLONEL: She was in no condition to be released. Our buildings are sanitary, Mister Kempler.

KEMPLER: May I use your telephone?

COLONEL: I'd rather you didn't.

KEMPLER: Colonel, I find these charges incredible to believe.

COLONEL: Yes, I can sympathize.

KEMPLER: Abril doesn't drink.

COLONEL: Perhaps there is more about her.

KEMPLER: I think not.

COLONEL: May I ask you something, Mister Kempler? *(Pause)* Why are you here?

KEMPLER: In Morocco?

COLONEL: Yes.

KEMPLER: Our jobs brought us here.

COLONEL: Please make it clear to me.

KEMPLER: You have our papers.

COLONEL: Is it that you like foreign food?

KEMPLER: Our work coincides often, and so we travel. My firm is building the industrial park outside your city.

COLONEL: Yes, I know that.

KEMPLER: Abril is with the affiliate bank.

COLONEL: Does she dress this way at the office?

KEMPLER: Obviously not.

COLONEL: Do they not pay her enough?

KEMPLER: Please don't sound ridiculous.

COLONEL: Do I?

KEMPLER: It is a gross distortion.

COLONEL: There is a serious epidemic in my country, and some precautions are needed.

KEMPLER: I can understand.

COLONEL: Not that we don't want foreign investors.

KEMPLER: Then why pick on my wife?

COLONEL: May I recite a parable? *(Phone rings; answering phone.) Na-on? ("Yes?". Listening) Sho-kun. ("Thank you". To* KEMPLER*)* Your wife had been checked for a contagion. She will be detained.

KEMPLER: You must let me see her.

COLONEL: For now that must wait.

KEMPLER: I insist.

COLONEL: You should make a friend of me, Mister Kempler. I am in a position to help you.

KEMPLER: I'm listening.

COLONEL: First, have a cigarette.

*(*KEMPLER *accepts one.)*

COLONEL: You needn't inhale to enjoy.

KEMPLER: What can I do for you?

COLONEL: *(Ignoring* KEMPLER*)* The tobacco is excellent. Almost sweet.

KEMPLER: Yes, very mild.

COLONEL: I keep them in a humidor.

KEMPLER: Very wise.

COLONEL: And yet my wife worries for me. Cancer scares.

KEMPLER: Can I write a check?

COLONEL: No, no, no. I wasn't looking for a gift, Mister Kempler. First of all, my commander would expect a percentage. Secondly, I would feel compromised and obligated. You might send other things in the mail. I could not in good conscience accept anything in this context. No, no, keep your checks. You are in the company of an honest officer.

KEMPLER: That is reassuring.

COLONEL: Furthermore, a bribe is a direct insult to Morocco.

KEMPLER: Colonel, I was not suggesting anything of the kind.

COLONEL: Bribes make soldiers complacent. Am I repeating myself? (Pause) Please, put aside your checkbook. We will do this the proper way.

KEMPLER: Fine.

COLONEL: Do you play chess?

KEMPLER: Why do you ask?

COLONEL: I am quite skillful at the game. And backgammon. Do you play backgammon, Mister Kempler?

KEMPLER: No.

COLONEL: Four-handed bridge?

KEMPLER: No, Colonel.

COLONEL: Did you play with little buildings as a boy?

KEMPLER: Please, we're wasting time.

COLONEL: Yes, I am sorry. (Pause) How is it that you married a whore?

KEMPLER: I will call the U.S. Consulate. *(Standing)*

COLONEL: But of course. *(Rising)* Thank you for stopping by, Mister Kempler.

DAY TWO

COLONEL: Good day, Mister Kempler.

KEMPLER: I have a letter from my Ambassador.

COLONEL: Is that so?

KEMPLER: Please... *(Handing it over)*

COLONEL: It's addressed to myself. And in his hand. *(Pause)* Why didn't he call? *(Pause)* Very well. *(Puts letter down without reading.)* What more can I do for you?

KEMPLER: Damn it, you can read the letter.

COLONEL: *(Obliging* KEMPLER*)* Yes, all right then. *(Pause)* But he makes no mention of venereal disease.

KEMPLER: Venereal disease?

COLONEL: Syphilis, yes.

KEMPLER: You will either release her, or let my doctor see her.

COLONEL: Bring in your doctor, Mister Kempler.

KEMPLER: I shall.

COLONEL: But I doubt that he will contest our reports.

KEMPLER: I hope this will cost you your rank.

COLONEL: Are you Jewish, Mister Kempler?

KEMPLER: What?

COLONEL: What is your religion?

KEMPLER: How does that matter?

COLONEL: Not in the slightest. But tell me.

KEMPLER: I've been overseas for fifteen years and have never experienced such idiocy.

COLONEL: I won't let you flatter me, Mister Kempler.

KEMPLER: Colonel, you are an idiot of some caliber.

COLONEL: We will become better friends in time.

KEMPLER: What do you hope to gain from this?

COLONEL: Perhaps your imagination is running away. I am not a sinister man. Look, here is a picture of my family. *(Shows photo on his desk)* I am hardworking. This office takes the worse abuse. Come now, have a cigarette.

KEMPLER: Why have you abducted my wife?

COLONEL: I have already told you.

KEMPLER: You dressed her and photographed her. It's all very entertaining. Who are you trying to hurt?

COLONEL: No one.

KEMPLER: Her bank has received complaints.

COLONEL: Yes, I have spoken directly with her officers.

KEMPLER: You are committing crimes against Americans.

COLONEL: I happen to like your nation.

KEMPLER: Then why this punishment?

COLONEL: Your wife was fraternizing with our army.

KEMPLER: This is very wrong.

COLONEL: *(Removing a sack from inside his desk.)* I have some of her personal things. You may wish to take them with you. *(Opening sack. Handling folded blouse delicately.)* She wears contact lenses. Have you a pair of glasses for her? *(Pause)* Perhaps you can bring them tomorrow.

KEMPLER: Please let me see her for one minute.

COLONEL: And suppose I should let you. What then? You would want her released on the spot. You would raise your voice and get in more difficulties with us. It is better to follow procedures.

KEMPLER: You're detaining an innocent woman.

COLONEL: What is your wish, Mister Kempler? Do you want her free? Do you want her well? Really, we can straighten this out with remarkable civility.

KEMPLER: I doubt it.

COLONEL: Then what do you suggest? I don't want your wife here. I am embarrassed to see you here. I don't want letters from your Embassy. Do you hear me clearly? Do you think we can try, Mister Kempler?

KEMPLER: I don't know.

COLONEL: You must at least trust me in this matter.

KEMPLER: I'd like to see my wife.

COLONEL: And you will.

KEMPLER: What did she do to warrant this?

COLONEL: Mrs Kempler was arrested for soliciting on the streets.

KEMPLER: Is it because she works at the bank?

COLONEL: I don't think so.

KEMPLER: You know of course it is an international bank.

COLONEL: Yes.

KEMPLER: It is a powerful bank.

COLONEL: I realize that.

KEMPLER: Is it my work then?

COLONEL: You put yourself in a curious position, Mister Kempler.

KEMPLER: My company's policies are very liberal here.

COLONEL: What are your company's policies?

KEMPLER: We hire locally. At least two-thirds. Few Algerians.

COLONEL: Are you Jewish, Mister Kempler?

KEMPLER: Why do you continue on that?

COLONEL: Because I don't like Jews.

KEMPLER: We appreciate these business opportunities in Fez.

COLONEL: Tell me what you are.

KEMPLER: Yes, I am Jewish.

COLONEL: I am not surprised.

KEMPLER: But my wife is not.

COLONEL: I am not an anti-Semite, Mister Kempler. My opinions are rather mild. *(Pause)* Is your architectural firm from New York?

KEMPLER: Yes.

COLONEL: But the names are not Jewish? *(Pause)* Somehow we're always doing business with Jews.

KEMPLER: We'll build more with time.

COLONEL: You make generous payments under the table to a long list of people. It is an interesting arrangement.

KEMPLER: Why did you stage those photographs?

COLONEL: What?

KEMPLER: They were staged.

COLONEL: Shall we discuss architecture? Are we really in store for American skyscrapers? What beautiful dreams have you waiting for us?

KEMPLER: The designs are very exciting.

COLONEL: Are we making you fat and bored? Why do you architects put bathrooms in the oddest of places? *(Pause)* Don't be silent with me.

KEMPLER: What would you like to hear?

COLONEL: What would I like to hear? Anything you care to say.

KEMPLER: You seem to know enough.

COLONEL: Then you should go back to your hotel and rehearse.

KEMPLER: Rehearse what?

COLONEL: Stories. Make up a story.

KEMPLER: I will.

COLONEL: That's good to hear. *(Pause)* Let us talk tomorrow. Good afternoon.

DAY THREE

COLONEL: I see that you have brought your physician.

KEMPLER: With your permission.

COLONEL: Yes, but of course.

KEMPLER: Is he with her now?

COLONEL: Yes.

KEMPLER: How is she?

COLONEL: Fine.

KEMPLER: Has she slept?

COLONEL: Yes.

KEMPLER: And eating?

COLONEL: I believe so.

KEMPLER: I will see her today.

COLONEL: You will wait.

KEMPLER: I have some of her things.

COLONEL: Leave them with me.

KEMPLER: And her glasses.

COLONEL: Thank you.

KEMPLER: I must have her home.

COLONEL: We will try.

KEMPLER: We are seldom apart.

COLONEL: I sympathize.

KEMPLER: Will there be a formal arraignment?

COLONEL: It has already occurred. *(Pause)* You will receive notice of the trial.

KEMPLER: How soon?

COLONEL: Perhaps in a few weeks.

KEMPLER: Must it go to trial?

COLONEL: I'm afraid so.

KEMPLER: Why is she being set up?

COLONEL: I cannot answer that.

KEMPLER: Our country has good relations with yours.

COLONEL: Yes.

KEMPLER: There must be a way to resolve this.

COLONEL: Return to your Consulate, Mister Kempler.

KEMPLER: Surely you could intervene?

COLONEL: I could not.

KEMPLER: And what if the doctor says that she is fine?

COLONEL: But she is not.

KEMPLER: God help you if you cause her pain.

COLONEL: She is being given penicillin.

KEMPLER: You better not fuck around with her.

COLONEL: Go home and get some sleep.

KEMPLER: I'll wait for the doctor.

COLONEL: Go home, Mister Kempler.

DAY FOUR

COLONEL: Did you know that we had to devalue our currency?

KEMPLER: I heard this morning.

COLONEL: It is unfortunate. Nothing keeps stable.

KEMPLER: Many countries have the same problem.

COLONEL: Thanks to the London economists, it is cheap to see Morocco.

KEMPLER: Yes, it is.

COLONEL: Now my salary will buy even less groceries for tomorrow. *(Pause)* How are your hotel accommodations?

KEMPLER: Sufficient.

COLONEL: We have remarkably fine hotels.

KEMPLER: Yes, I would agree.

COLONEL: Did your physician report back to you?

KEMPLER: Yes.

COLONEL: He corroborated with our doctors?

KEMPLER: Yes.

COLONEL: It needn't be a mystery.

KEMPLER: My wife is in your jail.

COLONEL: Only temporarily.

KEMPLER: The doctor said it is an early infection.

COLONEL: Yes, we caught it quickly.

KEMPLER: Your medics gave it to her.

COLONEL: No, Mister Kempler.

KEMPLER: She told my doctor they did.

COLONEL: Out of embarrassment, no doubt.

KEMPLER: You son-of-a-bitch.

COLONEL: Sit down, Mister Kempler

KEMPLER: Your fucking medics gave it to her.

COLONEL: Why ever should they?

KEMPLER: I demand to see her.

COLONEL: Let me tell you something, my friend. I met your wife on two occasions. She is quite beautiful. I would like to sleep with her myself.

KEMPLER: We should be able to strike a deal.

COLONEL: Not in that tone of voice.

KEMPLER: I don't understand you, Colonel.

COLONEL: Whisper to me, Mister Kempler.

KEMPLER: Go screw yourself.

COLONEL: You're not whispering.

KEMPLER: There's a limit to this business.

COLONEL: Why don't you contact Amnesty International?

KEMPLER: I have.

COLONEL: And the Red Cross.

KEMPLER: I have.

COLONEL: And your Ambassador calls me every day.

KEMPLER: I know why you're doing this.

COLONEL: Tell me, Mister Kempler.

KEMPLER: You're crazy.

COLONEL: Yes.

KEMPLER: Very crazy.

COLONEL: It's become a sporting thing.

KEMPLER: You find some prosperous Americans...

COLONEL: Please go on.

KEMPLER: And you play with their lives.

COLONEL: I am an officer in the King's army.

KEMPLER: How did you ever get to be Colonel?

COLONEL: I speak English.

KEMPLER: You are causing me great inconvenience.

COLONEL: That's putting it mildly. Why be so kind?

KEMPLER: Then you admit it.

COLONEL: Admit what?

KEMPLER: What you're doing to my wife.

COLONEL: Your wife is very well educated.

KEMPLER: What is that supposed to mean?

COLONEL: Our women are hardly schooled.

KEMPLER: Are you punishing her for that?

COLONEL: No.

KEMPLER: Then why bring it up?

COLONEL: My wife stays home with our children.

KEMPLER: Your nation is very backward.

COLONEL: My nation is based on tradition.

KEMPLER: Your people are illiterate.

COLONEL: I cannot argue that.

KEMPLER: But why snap at my wife?

COLONEL: Mister Kempler, I told you. I like your wife. *(Silence)* Tomorrow you may see her.

DAY FIVE

COLONEL: You are the first person I see each day.

KEMPLER: The privilege is mutual.

COLONEL: Did I make a promise to you?

KEMPLER: I believe so.

COLONEL: Then I won't keep you any further.

KEMPLER: Thank you.

COLONEL: You needn't thank me. *(Pause)* I see you decided to shave. *(Pause)* You look very presentable. *(Picks lint from* KEMPLER's *jacket.)*

KEMPLER: How much time do I get?

COLONEL: As long as you want. *(Pause)* Go right ahead, Mister Kempler.

*(*KEMPLER *hesitates with his exit. Some fear over meeting his wife.)*

DAY SIX

COLONEL: How good to see you, Mister Kempler. *(Pause)* We have the trial date.

KEMPLER: When?

COLONEL: Three weeks.

KEMPLER: Why so long?

COLONEL: It is the best we can do.

KEMPLER: What about bail?

COLONEL: No, I'm sorry.

KEMPLER: My Ambassador says there is no precedent for this detention.

COLONEL: Well, I think we shall work around it.

KEMPLER: My wife needs to see a dentist.

COLONEL: Did she request that?

KEMPLER: Yes.

COLONEL: All right then.

KEMPLER: She would like unsoiled clothes.

COLONEL: The wash is done weekly.

KEMPLER: I would like to give her some reading material.

COLONEL: She has magazines in her quarters.

KEMPLER: Please make her feel comfortable.

COLONEL: Yes, Mister Kempler.

KEMPLER: There are insects in her bed. *(Pause)* I would appreciate anything you can do.

COLONEL: Of course. She will get another bed.

KEMPLER: And paper for the lavatory.

COLONEL: Certainly.

KEMPLER: My Ambassador will be stopping by sometime today.

COLONEL: Thank you for telling me.

KEMPLER: And an American journalist.

COLONEL: Fine.

KEMPLER: How long will this go on?

COLONEL: Be patient if you can.

KEMPLER: It is wrong.

COLONEL: How are things at the Industrial Park?

KEMPLER: All right.

COLONEL: On schedule?

KEMPLER: Yes.

COLONEL: Do you walk around with a little lunch pail?

KEMPLER: I do.

COLONEL: Sit, Mister Kempler. Today let's make it a social visit.

KEMPLER: No, thank you.

COLONEL: When was the last time you slept with Mrs Kempler?

KEMPLER: Go to hell.

COLONEL: I'm only suggesting your good health.

KEMPLER: I've been examined.

COLONEL: That was prudent.

KEMPLER: No, my attorney suggested it.

COLONEL: Then you will appear in court.

KEMPLER: If need be.

COLONEL: The men in my command will support these charges quite graphically.

KEMPLER: Of course.

COLONEL: Take me seriously.

KEMPLER: Army life must suit you.

COLONEL: It is respectable.

KEMPLER: The stench permeates the uniform.

COLONEL: It is the King's army.

KEMPLER: How many women do you have locked away?

COLONEL: Not as many as Iran.

KEMPLER: But quite a bit.

COLONEL: A fair share.

KEMPLER: For solicitation?

COLONEL: In many instances.

KEMPLER: Do the convictions hold?

COLONEL: Ask your attorney.

KEMPLER: I'm asking you.

COLONEL: They hold.

KEMPLER: She's willing to leave the country.

COLONEL: Invariably.

KEMPLER: She's not like other women.

COLONEL: I hope not.

KEMPLER: They live on the streets.

COLONEL: There's a reflex in Moroccan life which attempts what I like to call human betterment. Penal life is part of that reflex.

KEMPLER: You don't care about these women.

COLONEL: But I do. I am a humanitarian.

KEMPLER: You are a racist, Colonel.

COLONEL: Am I?

KEMPLER: You know what I mean.

COLONEL: We are all children of Abraham.

KEMPLER: I think not.

COLONEL: One would like to believe it. *(Pause)* How do you reconcile yourself, Mister Kempler, spending your talents in the Arab world.

KEMPLER: I don't have to.

COLONEL: Certainly your have principles.

KEMPLER: Thank you for your time. *(About to leave)*

COLONEL: Your wife is of Arab descent, Mister Kempler. Did you know that?

DAY SEVEN

COLONEL: There will be a dentist coming this afternoon.

KEMPLER: How is she today?

COLONEL: In good spirits.

KEMPLER: Is she in a private cell?

COLONEL: Yes.

KEMPLER: My Ambassador said there will be some developments in the next few hours.

COLONEL: Did he say that?

KEMPLER: Yes.

COLONEL: He seems to be very influential in our city.

KEMPLER: It would be a good thing.

COLONEL: The Ambassador is a close acquaintance of the Commissioner.

KEMPLER: Is that a fact?

COLONEL: You have used your leverage, Mister Kempler.

KEMPLER: She's had enough of your hospitality.

COLONEL: And you're getting to be a nuisance. *(Pause)* There are some women here waiting for several years.

KEMPLER: I'm tired of waiting.

COLONEL: Go listen to some music. Leave, please.

KEMPLER: You will hear more from us.

COLONEL: A paperback about Morocco?

KEMPLER: You know, every dirty restaurant has a bit of you inside it. I see many men with your face.

COLONEL: Perhaps you ought to see a doctor.

KEMPLER: I'd like to see my wife now.

COLONEL: Yes, go right ahead.

KEMPLER: Thank you.

COLONEL: Today your wife confessed.

KEMPLER: Confessed?

COLONEL: To the charges.

KEMPLER: Why should she?

COLONEL: Because she is guilty.

KEMPLER: This is terribly wrong.

COLONEL: Would you like me to read her affidavit?

KEMPLER: No.

COLONEL: It's very short.

KEMPLER: I can imagine how you worded it.

COLONEL: Yes, well...I'll leave a copy with you.

(KEMPLER *reads and is quietly devastated.*)

COLONEL: This should expedite things.

KEMPLER: Did you bargain with her?

COLONEL: Why don't you ask your wife?

KEMPLER: I will.

COLONEL: And ask her if she was treated with respect.

KEMPLER: *(Pocketing affidavit)* Any other matter to settle?

COLONEL: You can see your wife now.

KEMPLER: Fine.

COLONEL: How is your building project?

KEMPLER: Why do you ask?

COLONEL: When is ribbon-cutting?

KEMPLER: Fairly soon.

COLONEL: Please do invite me.

KEMPLER: You are on my list.

COLONEL: How thoughtful.

KEMPLER: Aren't you ever given a day off?

COLONEL: It's a ten-day shift.

KEMPLER: You could stand a change of clothes.

COLONEL: Yes, forgive me.

KEMPLER: It's quite all right.

COLONEL: My wife is to blame. *(Pause)* She works very hard, Mister Kempler.

KEMPLER: Perhaps we could get together some afternoon for tea?

COLONEL: A very kind suggestion.

KEMPLER: Then after Abril is released.

COLONEL: If luck so has it.

KEMPLER: For a moment you can pretend that I'm not a Jew.

COLONEL: For a moment.

DAY EIGHT

KEMPLER: Renovation?

COLONEL: They're bringing indoor plumbing into the dormitories.

KEMPLER: It's a nice touch to the facility.

COLONEL: Yes, we think so.

KEMPLER: My country is beginning extradition proceedings. A change of venue.

COLONEL: God's speed to you.

KEMPLER: Her confession is void.

COLONEL: Is it?

KEMPLER: She copied it from your steno.

COLONEL: It is in plain English, and in her hand.

KEMPLER: She had no choice. *(Pause)* I hope you will stop annoying her with your impromptu visits. She's not starved for conversation.

COLONEL: A jailer must look after his guests. To lessen the loneliness of these long days. Am I not a bright conversationalist? I watch your wife through her prison window, I tap the door several times, I hand her a cigarette and a sweet pastry. Can you take issue with me on this?

(Noticing KEMPLER's *disdain)*

COLONEL: You exasperate me, Mister Kempler.

KEMPLER: I expect these incidents to end without further pain.

COLONEL: You will get your wish.

KEMPLER: I speak for my wife as you know.

COLONEL: You are a hero in my eyes. A cigarette?

KEMPLER: This time next week we will be in New York.

COLONEL: Be careful with us.

KEMPLER: Our memories of Fez will fall into the nearest sewer.

COLONEL: Her looseness is no reflection on my city.

KEMPLER: It is fiction.

COLONEL: Be careful that Mrs Kempler does not repeat herself in some other town.

KEMPLER: I don't think so. *(Pause)* I wish my country could extend to you the same hospitality you have shown to us.

COLONEL: That would be welcoming. We are both Semitic, in a manner of speaking.

KEMPLER: I wouldn't be cheerful about it.

COLONEL: Why not?

KEMPLER: Because it is a depressing picture.

COLONEL: Only if you think so.

KEMPLER: Your people have so many resources.

COLONEL: Your people too.

KEMPLER: But I'm talking about your natural resources, your lands.

COLONEL: You may build for us. I think that is fair.

KEMPLER: It isn't.

COLONEL: But it is American. Labor for contract.

KEMPLER: With good will.

COLONEL: If there is any...

KEMPLER: Someone ought to build a real facility instead of keeping this stable.

COLONEL: Why not bid for it?

KEMPLER: Next year.

COLONEL: Yes, when you visit us next year. *(Pause)* You and I make conversation easily.

KEMPLER: It is marvelous, Colonel.

COLONEL: I never know when you're joking, Mister Kempler.

DAY NINE

COLONEL: Sit down, Mister Kempler. I have the recent medic's report. *(Pause)* Her treatment is going accordingly and should cure her totally. No allergic reaction from the patient. Eating habits are normal. Her blood pressure is good. The dental work begun earlier in the week has been completed. Apparently they built a cap around one of the teeth. And that is our report. *(Pause)* Any questions?

KEMPLER: No.

COLONEL: Good.

KEMPLER: She'll be leaving tomorrow?

COLONEL: Luck is on your side.

KEMPLER: It is too long.

COLONEL: Think, in a few hours this will be over and you and your wife will be together.

KEMPLER: You're right.

COLONEL: You don't look happy, Mister Kempler.

KEMPLER: I am very happy.

COLONEL: How about smiling a little?

KEMPLER: I am smiling.

COLONEL: Let's have a celebration drink. *(Brings out bottle from desk)* These times are brief.

KEMPLER: Just a short one, thanks.

COLONEL: *L'chaim.*

KEMPLER: Same to you.

(COLONEL *and* KEMPLER *drink.*)

COLONEL: Another?

KEMPLER: No.

COLONEL: Must you hate me every morning?

KEMPLER: Yes.

COLONEL: *(Pours himself a second drink.)* You would like to cheat me?

KEMPLER: How could I cheat you?

COLONEL: You make more money than I. You dress well. You have a very exciting wife. You travel around the world.

KEMPLER: And you can rot in your jail.

COLONEL: Yes, exactly. I can rot in my jail.

KEMPLER: You elicit sympathy, Colonel.

COLONEL: Yes, I know. *(Laughing)* It's a jail full of fugitive women. Half of them were found on their back. I am their warden. I am their shepherd. *(Pause)* They have sad lives. You can understand.

KEMPLER: I'd like to see my wife now.

COLONEL: Let her wait a moment. *(Pause)* You won't be allowed physical contact with her for some time. You must be patient with her problem.

KEMPLER: Thank you for the advice.

COLONEL: You may hug her all you want.

KEMPLER: Thanks.

COLONEL: Kissing is at your discretion. *(Pause)* Have you any children?

KEMPLER: No.

COLONEL: I have six. My oldest is fourteen. He has my features. My son is very important to me. He has a temper like the devil.

KEMPLER: We wish your family well.

COLONEL: Do you plan to have a family?

KEMPLER: Perhaps.

COLONEL: Do you like baseball, Mister Kempler?

KEMPLER: Not too much.

COLONEL: It is a popular thing?

KEMPLER: Yes.

COLONEL: We have races here.

KEMPLER: What sort of races?

COLONEL: Dog races.

KEMPLER: I thought this was a religious city.

COLONEL: Would you like to join me for a race?

KEMPLER: What do you expect me to say?

COLONEL: Why do you always answer me with another question?

KEMPLER: I'd rather you show me a few of your mosques.

COLONEL: Unfortunately that is not permitted.

KEMPLER: I've seen the one in Meknes.

COLONEL: You must be Moslem to see the mosques.

KEMPLER: Why not arrange something for me?

COLONEL: Would you like an armband with a yellow star?

KEMPLER: No.

COLONEL: Why did you marry a Gentile?

KEMPLER: I have no answer.

COLONEL: Aren't you religious, Mister Kempler? I'm told that you are.

KEMPLER: No.

COLONEL: You get strident like a foolish zealot.

KEMPLER: No, not at all.

COLONEL: Have I created a zealot then?

KEMPLER: No.

COLONEL: Is it good to be a Jew?

KEMPLER: It is.

COLONEL: I can only wonder, Mister Kempler. *(Pause)* You seem to tell me so little. *(Pause)* Is this secrecy Jewish?

DAY TEN

COLONEL: Good day, Mister Kempler. *(Long silence)* Your wife is waiting for you in the next room.

END OF ACT ONE

ACT TWO

*(Some days later. Evening. An expensive restaurant in
Malaga, Spain. Tables on the terrace. Lights rise. Perhaps
there is Spanish guitar music.* KEMPLER *is downstage
lighting a cigarette. He sees* MRS KEMPLER *entering. He
joins her, smiles. A silence)*

KEMPLER: You were gone a long time.

MRS KEMPLER: I couldn't find the lavatory.

KEMPLER: I've ordered for you. *(Pause)* Clams.

MRS KEMPLER: Excellent.

KEMPLER: Salad. Local wine.

MRS KEMPLER: And you?

KEMPLER: Chateaubriand.

MRS KEMPLER: Is Ralph coming?

KEMPLER: No.

MRS KEMPLER: Really?

KEMPLER: He cancelled.

MRS KEMPLER: That's strange.

KEMPLER: He's under the weather. Left word with the
hotel desk.

MRS KEMPLER: I'm disappointed.

KEMPLER: So am I, darling.

MRS KEMPLER: Then shall we phone him afterwards?

KEMPLER: If you like.

MRS KEMPLER: Is it cool out here?

KEMPLER: Yes, take my jacket.

MRS KEMPLER: No, darling. I'll be all right.

KEMPLER: A cocktail?

MRS KEMPLER: No, I think not. What are you drinking?

KEMPLER: Vodka.

MRS KEMPLER: May I? *(Sipping)* How long are we going to stay?

KEMPLER: At the hotel?

MRS KEMPLER: It's a lovely hotel. The austere view of the harbor and the Plaza Del Toros. I love Spain in September, don't you?

KEMPLER: We'll stay a few more days. It's up to you.

MRS KEMPLER: Won't you need to get back this week?

KEMPLER: No, I made arrangements.

MRS KEMPLER: Still...

KEMPLER: Don't worry your little head.

MRS KEMPLER: I know your deadline, Charles.

(A WAITER enters, serves KEMPLER and MRS KEMPLER wine, exits. They hold up their glasses.)

KEMPLER: Shall we toast?

MRS KEMPLER: What will it be tonight?

KEMPLER: To good living.

MRS KEMPLER: Cheers.

(KEMPLER and MRS KEMPLER touch glasses, drink.)

MRS KEMPLER: I'm having the worst difficulty with my makeup this evening. Does it show?

KEMPLER: No, no.

MRS KEMPLER: But my mascara, Charles?

KEMPLER: Perhaps it's perspiration.

MRS KEMPLER: Not so loud.

KEMPLER: Aren't you feeling well?

MRS KEMPLER: Yes, I think so.

KEMPLER: Are you having chills?

MRS KEMPLER: Earlier. I'm fine now.

KEMPLER: We can stay in tonight.

MRS KEMPLER: Let's see, darling.

KEMPLER: Am I doting over you?

MRS KEMPLER: Of course not.

(KEMPLER *and* MRS KEMPLER *hold hands briefly.)*

KEMPLER: It becomes second nature for me.

MRS KEMPLER: A model husband you are.

KEMPLER: An inept model.

MRS KEMPLER: Are you fishing for sympathy?

KEMPLER: *(Playful)* Yes.

MRS KEMPLER: You can have anything from me, but sympathy.

KEMPLER: You're looking healthier, Mrs Kempler.

MRS KEMPLER: It's the wine.

KEMPLER: What would you like to do tomorrow?

MRS KEMPLER: The gardens at the Alcazaba?

KEMPLER: And afterwards?

MRS KEMPLER: Let's picnic and get drunk silly.

KEMPLER: I see you're feeling back in stride.

MRS KEMPLER: Some have jet lag. Perhaps it was jail lag. *(Touching her tooth)*

KEMPLER: The cap again?

MRS KEMPLER: The dental work was done by a gorilla.

KEMPLER: We could always have the work checked. *(Pause)* At least they didn't charge for it.

MRS KEMPLER: Oh, but they did.

KEMPLER: One cannot sue a foreign government.

MRS KEMPLER: Not if I could have my way.

KEMPLER: We'll put this behind us. A great story to tell our friends in the States. One day we'll have a good laugh over it. *(Pause)* They were getting to me through you.

MRS KEMPLER: Why?

KEMPLER: I had no business being there.

MRS KEMPLER: Darling, nothing was illegal.

KEMPLER: They knew my firm was Jewish, fronting through affiliates.

MRS KEMPLER: Morocco is not Syria, Charles.

KEMPLER: Every Arab nation plays games.

MRS KEMPLER: True.

KEMPLER: Are you upset with me?

MRS KEMPLER: No.

KEMPLER: I did everything humanly possible.

MRS KEMPLER: Perhaps had you offered cash, instead of a check...

KEMPLER: The banks were closed.

MRS KEMPLER: Or your Rolex...

KEMPLER: Perhaps. Who's to say? Perhaps I was too aggressive? I thought I did my best. *(Pause)* Where is the waiter?

MRS KEMPLER: It's a three star kitchen, Charles. When they're ready.

KEMPLER: We should have ordered in. Did you hear about your transfer?

MRS KEMPLER: Not yet.

KEMPLER: Will it be any problem?

MRS KEMPLER: Hardly.

KEMPLER: What's your preference? You needn't work everything around me.

MRS KEMPLER: Whatever darling.

KEMPLER: We can stay in Europe.

MRS KEMPLER: Fine.

KEMPLER: Or Japan.

MRS KEMPLER: I really don't care.

KEMPLER: Well, I'd just as soon stay in the Mediterrean.

MRS KEMPLER: One telegram would suffice.

KEMPLER: You do have more flexibility.

MRS KEMPLER: We just have to buy some more summer clothes.

KEMPLER: A more conservative look.

MRS KEMPLER: Fashion first.

KEMPLER: Leave cleavage to the ladies in Vegas.

MRS KEMPLER: And what about my umbrage?

KEMPLER: I'm so hungry this evening.

MRS KEMPLER: Have another drink.

KEMPLER: Why do you encourage me?

MRS KEMPLER: Because you're different when you drink.

KEMPLER: Different than what?

MRS KEMPLER: Different than sober.

KEMPLER: Why can't I be sober?

MRS KEMPLER: We're on holiday...

(WAITER *enters, serves appetizers.* KEMPLER *and* MRS KEMPLER *sit at table.*)

KEMPLER: It's peculiar how Arabs drink everywhere but in public sight. Hemp in their cigarettes. Their hidden nightclubs...

MRS KEMPLER: It's a veiled society. They mask vice artfully.

KEMPLER: And they know how to protect their women.

MRS KEMPLER: Yes, like beloved livestock. I don't want to discuss the inanities of the Arab world.

KEMPLER: The wisdom of inanities.

MRS KEMPLER: To find women displaced under the peasants, who are under the merchants and militia, who are under the politically affluent...makes me very ashamed of my background. This casual degradation has become all too embarrassing, particularly when it hits home, Charles.

KEMPLER: I thought you were immune to it.

MRS KEMPLER: If only I were...

KEMPLER: I'll never forget his odor.

MRS KEMPLER: The Colonel?

KEMPLER: His wonderfully cheap tobacco and dank-mold carpets. He knew I found him abhorrent. For his dirtiness, above all.

MRS KEMPLER: Yes, darling, you see...cleanliness is looked upon as a very alien characteristic. Grounds for suspicion and deportation. Unless one is very religious.

KEMPLER: They all say they're religious.

MRS KEMPLER: Even peasants want respect.

KEMPLER: He was a peasant.

MRS KEMPLER: For a peasant, he spoke excellent English. *(Pause)* I really believed he liked you, Charles.

KEMPLER: Liked me?

MRS KEMPLER: He spoke highly of you. Admired your suits. Enjoyed your humor. Oh, he was a little crazy. You can understand that. How often does a jailor catch an American? When he talked to me in Arabic, he forgot his rank. You didn't cause him offense.

KEMPLER: He told you so?

MRS KEMPLER: Yes.

KEMPLER: What else did he tell you?

MRS KEMPLER: Very little else.

KEMPLER: They've kept the photographs.

MRS KEMPLER: I really don't know.

KEMPLER: How many were there?

MRS KEMPLER: Men? I thought we weren't going to discuss this another time.

KEMPLER: Everything you told me in jail was contradictory.

MRS KEMPLER: I had a terrible fever then.

KEMPLER: Why do you bring up inconsistencies?

MRS KEMPLER: Talk to my doctor, Charles.

KEMPLER: I have talked with him.

MRS KEMPLER: Wonderful.

KEMPLER: What am I to think?

MRS KEMPLER: Think what you want. Thank God I survived Morocco.

KEMPLER: I have thanked God.

MRS KEMPLER: I wish I could believe you.

KEMPLER: I have thanked God.

MRS KEMPLER: I know exactly what you went through.

KEMPLER: Do you?

MRS KEMPLER: I do.

KEMPLER: Doubts don't comfort me.

MRS KEMPLER: I don't sleep around. You think I do.

KEMPLER: That's not the issue.

MRS KEMPLER: What is the issue?

KEMPLER: I don't know, Abril.

MRS KEMPLER: Charles...

(KEMPLER *looks at* MRS KEMPLER *keenly.*)

MRS KEMPLER: Our marriage is very strong. To hell with everything else. You must believe that. *(Pause)* The photographs continue to bother you.

KEMPLER: Yes.

MRS KEMPLER: You know what choice they gave me.

KEMPLER: What choice did they give you?

MRS KEMPLER: *(Dryly)* Use your imagination.

KEMPLER: I'd rather not.

MRS KEMPLER: I was harassed on the street by their soldiers. It was nothing more than that. I was alone. One of their soldiers mistook me for something I wasn't. Everything was contrived to protect him. A little fiction goes a long way in Fez.

KEMPLER: You don't have to defend yourself.

MRS KEMPLER: Thank you.

KEMPLER: Everything was divisive.

MRS KEMPLER: Perhaps that was the point.

KEMPLER: Why were you at the bar?

MRS KEMPLER: Drinking, of course.

KEMPLER: Couldn't you have waited for a girlfriend?

MRS KEMPLER: I was working late that evening. And so were you.

KEMPLER: Why did you provoke the soldiers?

MRS KEMPLER: I don't like being followed into the Medina.

KEMPLER: In Morocco you told me a different story.

MRS KEMPLER: Did I?

KEMPLER: You said the incident started at the bank office.

MRS KEMPLER: I was targetted, Charles. Leave it at that.

KEMPLER: I'd like a better explanation.

MRS KEMPLER: Do I take an oath before answering?

KEMPLER: Please.

MRS KEMPLER: Sleep with cockroaches for a month, then ask me any question you want.

KEMPLER: Don't make a game of it.

MRS KEMPLER: It was not a game, Charles.

KEMPLER: The photographs don't show an inhibited woman.

MRS KEMPLER: What do they show?

KEMPLER: An unforgettable licentiousness.

MRS KEMPLER: (*Rising from table in anger*) You can't say that, Charles. I can't bear the hurt.

KEMPLER: Did they drug you? Why was it so difficult to see you?

MRS KEMPLER: You know the jails. Maybe I was unconscious. I was in a state of fright. *(Pause)* Do you think you married a prostitute?

KEMPLER: Don't be absurd.

MRS KEMPLER: Does it give you a vicarious thrill?

KEMPLER: Abril!

MRS KEMPLER: It's true, Charles. We seem to feed each other's lurid fantasies.

KEMPLER: I don't like punishment.

MRS KEMPLER: Nor do I. These last few days, I feel like a stranger to myself. *(Pause)* Why are you staring at me?

KEMPLER: I'm not the one to comment on moral conduct.

MRS KEMPLER: Why don't you?

KEMPLER: Because I'm more caught up on your motives.

MRS KEMPLER: My motives?

KEMPLER: Your hedonism. Your exhibitionism and contempt for social rules. You'll always be promiscuous. Since the first day I've known you.

MRS KEMPLER: I did not sleep with the Moroccan army. Even at gunpoint.

KEMPLER: Then my thinking is very twisted.

MRS KEMPLER: Obviously.

KEMPLER: Give me a sign, Abril, something to hold on to.

MRS KEMPLER: No vaccine in the world could withstand a Moroccan soldier. No vaccine could immune you from your worst fears. We can only make do with what we now have. I love you, Charles. Think of the bright side. They were very considerate. We can have relations again.

KEMPLER: Yes, it's remarkably accommodating of them. *(Spills drink.)* Damn it!

MRS KEMPLER: Have another then.

KEMPLER: It's just as well.

MRS KEMPLER: You believe I was whoring.

KEMPLER: Yes, I do.

MRS KEMPLER: To what purpose?

KEMPLER: Kicks.

MRS KEMPLER: Like taking drugs?

KEMPLER: Like fucking soldiers.

MRS KEMPLER: That's enough! *(Getting her composure)* My breeding's better than yours. I was at Oxford, darling.

KEMPLER: You're part Arab.

MRS KEMPLER: We're supreme racehorses and mythmakers.

KEMPLER: I tip my hat to you.

MRS KEMPLER: And I'm part Spanish. A double import. From both sides of the Mediterranean.

KEMPLER: A sterling combination.

MRS KEMPLER: How long do you intend to chaff?

KEMPLER: How long do you intend to embarrass us?

MRS KEMPLER: Indefinitely.

KEMPLER: Wonderful.

MRS KEMPLER: What sort of guarantee are you looking for?

KEMPLER: Fidelity being outside your vocabulary, any guarantee could only extend ninety days at best.

MRS KEMPLER: You don't know the limit of my vocabulary. You don't know my capacity for change. You're really not being fair to me. You don't know the pain I feel.

KEMPLER: I do.

MRS KEMPLER: Then why these doubts?

KEMPLER: You were on good terms with the Colonel.

MRS KEMPLER: I needed an ally in that hovel.

KEMPLER: Do you know what the Ambassador asked me?

MRS KEMPLER: Yes, you told me.

KEMPLER: "Mister Kempler, wives overseas often need mad money. Does your wife indulge herself after hours? *(Pause)* "Mister Kempler, your wife is most... charming." *(Pause)* "Mister Kempler, do you think you can keep an eye on her for the weeks ahead?"

(WAITER *enters with entrees.*)

MRS KEMPLER: Are you looking for a moral, Charles? What exactly is the point?

(WAITER *leaves, after catching a fleeting glance from her.*)

KEMPLER: If we lived in a small town, gossip would dampen your spirits.

MRS KEMPLER: I don't like small towns.

KEMPLER: So we wander like globetrotters.

MRS KEMPLER: Haven't you had an affair in the last year or two?

KEMPLER: *(Perhaps a lie)* No.

MRS KEMPLER: You wouldn't tell me anyway.

KEMPLER: You'd know the moment I do. I can't lie.

MRS KEMPLER: Oh, you lie famously.

KEMPLER: Not to you.

MRS KEMPLER: How would I know?

KEMPLER: Because you're more skillful at it.

MRS KEMPLER: Are we going to dine, or argue?

KEMPLER: I have no appetite. You've made me a laughingstock.

MRS KEMPLER: No one is laughing at you.

KEMPLER: *(Painfully)* They are laughing at me.

MRS KEMPLER: *(Tenderly, touching his hand)* Charles...

KEMPLER: *(After a pause, softly)* I'm so very much in love with you.

MRS KEMPLER: Keep telling me that.

KEMPLER: You can be so beautiful.

MRS KEMPLER: And so can you. I will behave better, darling.

KEMPLER: With each promise, there is a false star overhead.

MRS KEMPLER: Are you now counting stars?

KEMPLER: I am.

MRS KEMPLER: *(Coyly)* Count sheep, Charles. You were once extremely romantic.

KEMPLER: In the Peace Corps.

MRS KEMPLER: Not that many years ago.

KEMPLER: Before I started greying.

MRS KEMPLER: Success has affected you, darling.

KEMPLER: Why do you say that?

MRS KEMPLER: There was a time when you gave me special attention.

KEMPLER: Fatigue is a very human thing.

MRS KEMPLER: Is it really fatigue? *(Pause)* I can't have children. You know that pains me.

KEMPLER: As well as me.

MRS KEMPLER: Perhaps it's harder for the woman. We can go to all the expensive doctors in the world. It won't remedy the situation.

KEMPLER: Wanting children can be an act of will.

MRS KEMPLER: Which puts the onus on me.

KEMPLER: No.

MRS KEMPLER: I knew all my life that I would be childless. Since I was a little girl. I knew I would be refused customary things others are granted. I was marked early. Should I cry about it? Isn't it better that we just spend money on ourselves?

KEMPLER: We don't need money.

MRS KEMPLER: What a pity not to be broke and hungry, without a prayer in all hell. *(Pause. Kicking off her shoes)* My head is full of nonsense. Charles, are you going to make love to me tonight?

KEMPLER: Do I need a reservation?

MRS KEMPLER: *(Laughing)* Oh, yes.

KEMPLER: Is there a room assignment?

MRS KEMPLER: You know the room.

KEMPLER: Did you speak to the Colonel like that? *(Seeing his wife flustered)* Did you fall in love with him?

MRS KEMPLER: Charles, piss on your obsessions. *(Pause)* I think we ought to establish some rules between us. Either we are on holiday, or revisiting *Judgement At Nuremberg*.

KEMPLER: We are on holiday. *(He makes a conciliatory gesture.)*

MRS KEMPLER: Glory be to Heaven.

KEMPLER: Yes, glory be to Heaven. Have we failed each other?

MRS KEMPLER: No worse than other couples.

KEMPLER: I've lost the gift of forgiveness.

MRS KEMPLER: Under the circumstances I can understand. Let's elope again. Let's lose ourselves, Charles. Let's re-invent ourselves. Let's fall in love with our better parts.

KEMPLER: You're sincere.

MRS KEMPLER: I am.

KEMPLER: Nothing in my life prepared me for you, Abril.

MRS KEMPLER: As it should be.

KEMPLER: *(Suddenly amused)* I told Ralph.

MRS KEMPLER: You told Ralph what?

KEMPLER: About the arrest.

MRS KEMPLER: He must have had a good laugh.

KEMPLER: He did.

MRS KEMPLER: Wasn't Ralph's wife arrested?

KEMPLER: Yes, cocaine.

MRS KEMPLER: You and Ralph ought to start a club.

KEMPLER: We're working on it.

MRS KEMPLER: Do you want a divorce, Charles?

KEMPLER: No.

MRS KEMPLER: Are you certain?

KEMPLER: I'm in love with you.

MRS KEMPLER: Do you think I'm schizophrenic?

KEMPLER: Yes.

MRS KEMPLER: My problem is not hopeless.

KEMPLER: I could always rent you out to parties.

MRS KEMPLER: Charles, are you in a good mood today?

KEMPLER: Yes, I think so.

MRS KEMPLER: That's good. When you're in a good mood, I'm in a good mood.

KEMPLER: Then we should leave right now.

MRS KEMPLER: I haven't touched my plate.

KEMPLER: We should pack and fly out tonight.

MRS KEMPLER: Leave Spain?

KEMPLER: Damn it, let's buy a house in Massachusetts.

MRS KEMPLER: That is so dull, Charles.

KEMPLER: You owe me this.

MRS KEMPLER: There are limits.

KEMPLER: Why the hell do we have to live like gypsies?

MRS KEMPLER: Because I'm part gypsy.

KEMPLER: You're a little of everything. Your father warned me about spending twelve consecutive months with you. You had him around your finger too. After our wedding, he sent a letter covered with his tears. What did he know, that I don't.

MRS KEMPLER: *(Avoiding argument)* I really wish Ralph were here tonight. He would arbitrate for us. Every couple needs an arbitrator.

KEMPLER: Shall we ask the waiter?

MRS KEMPLER: Do what you want darling.

KEMPLER: How do they let you stay on at the bank?

MRS KEMPLER: I'm very good there.

KEMPLER: But they're reserved people.

MRS KEMPLER: And so am I.

KEMPLER: And the Pope is Jewish.

MRS KEMPLER: Is he, Charles? I never know when you're joking. *(Pause)* Are we candidates for therapy?

KEMPLER: Exemplary candidates.

MRS KEMPLER: I'm willing, if you are.

KEMPLER: You would end up sleeping with the psychiatrist.

MRS KEMPLER: Darling, are we a vaudeville?

KEMPLER: It seems so. Have you slept with Ralph?

MRS KEMPLER: Why do you ask that?

KEMPLER: Sixth sense.

MRS KEMPLER: I find it insulting.

KEMPLER: Answer me. Abril...

MRS KEMPLER: *(Ambiguously)* Once.

KEMPLER: Is that all?

MRS KEMPLER: Yes, I believe so.

KEMPLER: *(Slow burn)* Then what am I getting all working up about?

MRS KEMPLER: I've no idea.

KEMPLER: I feel murderous.

MRS KEMPLER: Take up golf, darling.

KEMPLER: Why don't you get out your appointment calendar and tell me the nights you're free.

MRS KEMPLER: Be a sport, Charles. You know my sense of humor.

KEMPLER: You make me cry inside.

MRS KEMPLER: You're very touching when you cry.

KEMPLER: Do you pity me?

MRS KEMPLER: Whatever for?

KEMPLER: For my masochism.

MRS KEMPLER: You?

KEMPLER: Me.

MRS KEMPLER: No, I don't pity you.

KEMPLER: Do you ever admire me?

MRS KEMPLER: At certain moments, yes. When you drive with the top down. When you toss your anxieties to the wind.

KEMPLER: Are we competing with each other?

MRS KEMPLER: These are too many questions for one night.

MRS KEMPLER: Have another drink. For me?

KEMPLER: There was a time in my life when I had tremendous discipline. Do you remember?

MRS KEMPLER: Are you over the hill now?

KEMPLER: It occurred to me.

MRS KEMPLER: Can I tell you the truth, Charles? *(Pause)* You are no longer modern.

KEMPLER: What is that supposed to mean?

MRS KEMPLER: I think you're closer to the last century. A Victorian caught in the wrong period. You want me to say cruel things. I can be no crueler than this. Strange, that an architect driven by innovation lives with those from the distant past. You are a bit of a relic. An antique. A very vulnerable heart.

KEMPLER: You're just as vulnerable.

MRS KEMPLER: In some ways.

KEMPLER: I can bruise you.

MRS KEMPLER: Yes, you could.

KEMPLER: Yet, I'm no harsher than you. Why must we hurt each other so?

MRS KEMPLER: I don't know, darling. Such things are never simple.

KEMPLER: Your time in jail has softened you. You seem to have acquired something useful.

MRS KEMPLER: Have I?

(KEMPLER *and* MRS KEMPLER *kiss slowly, passionately.*)

KEMPLER: *(After a pause)* God knows how much I love you.

MRS KEMPLER: And I...you. Let Morocco fade away. Or we'll go absolutely mad.

KEMPLER: I'll return in a few days.

MRS KEMPLER: But Charles...

KEMPLER: The complex is planned to open shortly. You understand.

MRS KEMPLER: We can both go back.

KEMPLER: You remember what the State Department said.

MRS KEMPLER: Yes, well, if that is what you want.

KEMPLER: Our luck has been perverse all year. *(Pause)* Call Ralph for me.

MRS KEMPLER: And say what?

KEMPLER: That I'll be out of town.

MRS KEMPLER: Are you being provocative?

KEMPLER: No.

MRS KEMPLER: You view Ralph as a rival.

KEMPLER: Not at all.

MRS KEMPLER: I know you better.

KEMPLER: Call Ralph and say that I know more than I should.

MRS KEMPLER: But why?

KEMPLER: Let's save our marriage as though our lives were at stake.

MRS KEMPLER: As you wish.

KEMPLER: I can't do it alone.

MRS KEMPLER: No one is expecting you to.

KEMPLER: You're so exceptionally bright and gifted, dearest. At times the loveliest woman in creation. I can't fault you for certain excesses, and who am I to make rules for a spirit such as yours.

MRS KEMPLER: Why Charles, that is so sweet of you to say.

KEMPLER: Therefore, I beg you to feign a little modesty for the next few months. Perhaps you'll get addicted to it. Something glorious might come of it. What do you think?

MRS KEMPLER: I think you are very generous.

KEMPLER: *(Pause)* Do you love me, Abril?

MRS KEMPLER: *(Touchingly direct)* Yes.

KEMPLER: Should I believe you?

MRS KEMPLER: Yes.

KEMPLER: Is the future bright?

MRS KEMPLER: The future is always bright.

KEMPLER: Things in the past are forgiven?

MRS KEMPLER: Best they are.

KEMPLER: I was never shocked.

MRS KEMPLER: I could swear that you were.

KEMPLER: No. I was never shocked. *(Takes out wallet, drops American Express card on check plate.)*

END OF ACT TWO

ACT THREE

(A week later. The COLONEL'*s office in Morocco.* KEMPLER *is at the door, waiting for the* COLONEL'*s attention.)*

KEMPLER: *(Abruptly, wired)* Excuse me, I thought you were free for the evening.

COLONEL: Yes, I thought so as well. Come in, Mister Kempler. I really didn't expect you to drop by. When you phoned, I was quite surprised.

KEMPLER: I thought it best to phone.

COLONEL: I'm honored that you called. You've been in my thoughts for several days. Come in, come in.

*(*KEMPLER *approaches the* COLONEL.*)*

COLONEL: Tell me, what are you doing here?

KEMPLER: Details.

COLONEL: I thought you left the country?

KEMPLER: Yes, for a short while. We were in Spain.

COLONEL: *(Patronizing)* And how was Spain?

KEMPLER: Quite beguiling actually. May I sit?

*(*COLONEL *gestures.)*

KEMPLER: I see you've painted the office.

COLONEL: Can you tell?

KEMPLER: A fine improvement.

COLONEL: Thank you. My wife chose the color. *(Pause)* Are you here strictly on business?

KEMPLER: The park has opened.

COLONEL: I was waiting for your invitation.

KEMPLER: You didn't miss a thing.

COLONEL: And now what, Mister Kempler?

KEMPLER: Plans on the continent. Too early to tell. *(Long pause. Awkward)* My office forwarded your letter.

COLONEL: What letter?

KEMPLER: I should say, your little note.

COLONEL: I sent no note.

KEMPLER: Is that right, Colonel? It was prison stationery.

COLONEL: Mister Kempler, I have no cause to do such a thing.

KEMPLER: I'm sure you had your reasons.

COLONEL: Reasons?

KEMPLER: Why belabor an unfortunate situation?

COLONEL: You must be dreaming.

KEMPLER: Not at all. My wife must also be dreaming.

COLONEL: I've had a very long day, Mister Kempler.

KEMPLER: My wife had me see a psychiatrist in Malaga.

COLONEL: Bravo!

KEMPLER: He was quite expensive. Three hundred dirhams a session. I didn't even get full hours.

COLONEL: Why are you telling me this?

KEMPLER: May I smoke?

COLONEL: By all means.

KEMPLER: Colonel, stop these little games.

COLONEL: Mister Kempler, I've no idea what the hell you're talking about. What games?

KEMPLER: Perhaps I've no tolerance for these things.

COLONEL: I'm a very busy man, from early in the morning. I try to make it easy for myself, and for others. If your building project is finished, why be here at all? Why imagine things that are not so? Why make faces at me, Mister Kempler? Why not just have a drink with me? *(Pause)* You look terrible. Are you well?

KEMPLER: Yes, of course.

COLONEL: Is your wife with you?

KEMPLER: Yes, she is.

COLONEL: How is she?

KEMPLER: Fine. Lovely as ever.

COLONEL: I didn't expect you to return to Fez. I thought you had made that clear to me.

KEMPLER: Perhaps I came back on principle.

COLONEL: Excuse me. *(Takes out liquor)* A drink?

KEMPLER: Please.

COLONEL: What can I do for you then?

KEMPLER: Tell me who my wife is?

COLONEL: Your wife is your wife.

KEMPLER: Why not amplify that for me?

COLONEL: Don't be ridiculous, Mister Kempler. You know your wife much better than I.

KEMPLER: In your note you had no trouble expressing yourself.

COLONEL: Was this note signed by me?

KEMPLER: I'm certain it was yours, Colonel.

COLONEL: And if it was mine, why would you be upset?

KEMPLER: Do I look upset?

COLONEL: What did this note say?

KEMPLER: *(Temper rising)* I worked very hard in Fez. Everyone knows that. I made time for her. We had more than enough time for each other. I know how to be generous.

COLONEL: Are you in trouble?

KEMPLER: Can I have another drink?

COLONEL: Take the bottle.

KEMPLER: *(Pouring from the bottle)* I trust your judgment. Did you know that?

COLONEL: My judgment, Mister Kempler?

KEMPLER: Tell me, just friend to friend, how would you continue with Abril?

COLONEL: I?

KEMPLER: Would you let her stay the way she was?

COLONEL: Your wife is a gypsy. I don't understand gypsies.

KEMPLER: But you speak her language.

COLONEL: I'm sure she speaks many languages.

KEMPLER: You know her for what she is. A woman like Abril can live without shame. I cannot.

COLONEL: Did you catch her again?

KEMPLER: Yes. Now I can tell by which earrings she has on. Isn't that something? The drop pearls are her little neon lights.

COLONEL: Are you being facetious?

KEMPLER: My wife is an anomaly. Hardly an asset. What would you do in this instance?

COLONEL: What instance?

KEMPLER: You found her with a...

COLONEL: *(Interrupting)* I cannot say.

KEMPLER: Shall I read your mind, Colonel?

COLONEL: Please.

KEMPLER: You would take down your saber. You would torture her, as you did in your jail.

COLONEL: Torture is arcane. You have a strange imagination, Mister Kempler.

KEMPLER: You would humiliate her beyond need or satisfaction. You would bond her, and brand her like cattle, keep her on a straw mattress without clothes. You would beat her and taunt her with your black riding crop. I know what you really can do, Colonel. Arabs dominate these bitches very well.

COLONEL: You watch too many movies, Mister Kempler.

KEMPLER: But it's true. These are your priorities. Two Arab brothers would sooner kill a woman, than let her come between them. That is your culture since creation.

COLONEL: Why overpraise my people? We're all thieves and beggars, addicts and murderers. *(Amused)* And you are Dagwood Bumstead. Isn't that so?

KEMPLER: Yes, I am.

COLONEL: It's a comic strip. You sleep on the couch, and the dog barks, and your wife Blondie has purchased a new dress with your seventeen credit cards. *(Pause)* Would you care for another drink? *(Pours two glasses.)* Yet your wife Blondie loves you very much. You must know that.

KEMPLER: I don't think so.

COLONEL: You are fooling yourself. Believe me, you are. My religion believes in duty with regard to the wife. She is not a kitchen appliance. She is not disposable as such. But training is expected, and you must do the training. How is that for wisdom?

KEMPLER: Uninspiring.

COLONEL: Yes, forgive me. I am not Mohammed.

KEMPLER: Your advice is late in coming.

COLONEL: And so is the Messiah.

KEMPLER: I cannot afford a shattered marriage. Can you understand that?

COLONEL: You are very gifted, Mister Kempler. I think you could sustain injury. You have plenty of nerve.

KEMPLER: Do you think so?

COLONEL: If you Jews charade with Gentile names and Gentile faces and Gentile firms, I call that nerve. Nerve to appear unquestionably Jewish. That you worked on your diction and that you admire our mosques and restaurants and women. Nerve to marry one of us, in fact. Yes, you have this incredible trait every waking day. It makes you successful, Mister Kempler. It's in your every step.

KEMPLER: Thank you for the ridicule.

COLONEL: It is a bouquet to you. *(Pause)* Where is your wife, Mister Kempler?

KEMPLER: I left her in Spain.

COLONEL: Is she well?

KEMPLER: I don't really care.

COLONEL: You do care.

KEMPLER: No, it's over.

COLONEL: Infidelity can be treated.

KEMPLER: I don't have a claim to her any longer.

COLONEL: Even whores have a state of grace.

KEMPLER: She's another species altogether.

COLONEL: Have children. That is my recommendation. Make babies. A half a dozen to start. *(Pause. Studied look)* It is heartfelt, Mister Kempler.

KEMPLER: We can't have children.

COLONEL: *(Sympathetic)* I'm sorry. *(Distracted, perhaps with papers on the desk)* How many men do you think have been with her?

KEMPLER: There were a good many.

COLONEL: Fifty? A hundred?

KEMPLER: Have you a bet with someone?

COLONEL: I'm only trying to get a grasp.

KEMPLER: She's not for hire. She never was.

COLONEL: I didn't insinuate anything.

KEMPLER: I'm not old-fashioned, Colonel.

COLONEL: You're simply a husband.

KEMPLER: Yes, I'm simply a husband. *(Long pause)* I threatened to kill her the night before leaving Malaga.

COLONEL: Did you?

KEMPLER: Our sex life stopped dead.

COLONEL: Was there a sex life at all, Mister Kempler?

KEMPLER: Yes.

COLONEL: No, no, you can tell me the truth...

KEMPLER: I am.

COLONEL: Are you faithful?

KEMPLER: She cheats. I do not cheat.

COLONEL: We all cheat. *(Pause)* Your wife is from Gibraltar. Once a crazy place. I wish I could be more helpful, Mister Kempler.

KEMPLER: Actually, you've been very helpful.

COLONEL: Have I?

KEMPLER: I thought you knew that.

COLONEL: I know very little.

KEMPLER: You know me like a glove. I admire you, Colonel. I admire your sense of resolve, and your polite manner. You have a circumspect mind too, and that has not gone by unnoticed. *(Pause)* I would like the photographs back, Colonel.

COLONEL: Yes, as you wish. *(Some physical contact with* KEMPLER*)* But first, why don't we go into the city tonight? You did invite me out. I know a very fine restaurant, Mister Kempler, with a Sephardic menu. We'll pretend we're two bachelors.

KEMPLER: Why pretend?

COLONEL: You are in a humor. *(Rising)* I'll get my coat. Has your wife been to see the project?

KEMPLER: She was reluctant to go. Sometimes she is superstitious.

COLONEL: Really?

KEMPLER: Women are superstitious, Colonel. You know that. I hope to carry on another project or two on the continent. Tangier. You know how good steady work can be.

COLONEL: I do.

KEMPLER: There's a building recession in my country. Architects must travel. I've come to accept this.

Jewish professionals with Berlitz dictionaries and loose cash in their suit pockets. Still, I believe in my profession. Architecture is a benign discipline. Art and engineering. Soul and body. Private and public. Do you see the connection?

COLONEL: No, Mister Kempler.

KEMPLER: The events over the last few weeks have shaken me. My training hasn't prepared me for you. I thought work was everything. What makes an architect happy? Posterity? Pomposity? We crown ourselves with each difficult creation. Your degree of understanding has moved me. You offer something remedial to my marriage. Your jealousy tipped me off to things, Colonel.

COLONEL: My jealousy?

KEMPLER: If I could lie as skillfully as you, I would be much stronger. I could reverse the damage I've incurred here. I could preserve the shine to my good name. *(Pause)* In the Medina, all the faces are shrouded in anonymity and mystery. I want my face to be branded in your presence. Burned onto your retina.

COLONEL: Clearly, I've offended you, my friend. I thought all was—as you call—judicious and fair. Is there something in this office for you?

KEMPLER: In this office...no.

COLONEL: Then my hands are tied.

KEMPLER: Talk to me.

COLONEL: Dear God, I am talking to you. If I rip your tongue out, Mister Kempler, you would still get in the last word. Isn't that so?

KEMPLER: What would you say if I told you...

COLONEL: Tell me what?

KEMPLER: If I told you that Mrs. Kempler has disappeared?

COLONEL: Has she? Where has she gone?

KEMPLER: Don't you know? Haven't you been communicating with her?

COLONEL: Mister Kempler, shall I call the police?

KEMPLER: You are the police.

COLONEL: If the woman has disappeared...

KEMPLER: Don't be clever.

COLONEL: Is she in this city?

KEMPLER: I don't know. We came back together.

COLONEL: That wasn't wise to bring her back, Mister Kempler.

KEMPLER: I had no choice. She couldn't bear the separation. What was I to do? Lock her in room until Fez was completed? She had something to prove to me. She needed to erase the traces of the scandal. I bought her jewelry. She gave it away to the valet. When the testing stopped, the teasing began. She told the chambermaid in Malaga that I was incontinent. That she had to throw away the sheets. This is her sense of humor. A luxury hotel, no less.

COLONEL: Are you incontinent?

KEMPLER: *(Ironic)* I have never wet a bed in my life.

COLONEL: Why did you marry this woman?

KEMPLER: I don't know. One would think it was from love. I was glad to break from my family, as she broke from hers. She vanquished things mediocre inside me.

COLONEL: She is an instrument of your daily embarrassment. Is this American, Mister Kempler? Mixing success with the best cow manure? You have magnificent dreams of erecting buildings and parks and monuments, dignity very few men achieve. But in all the time I have known you, I cannot see your dignity.

KEMPLER: Look harder, Colonel. It is there.

COLONEL: You're a stubborn man. As stubborn as she.

KEMPLER: No one spotted her as you had. No one at her office suspected.

COLONEL: They are all whores at the bank.

KEMPLER: I always thought of her as my princess.

COLONEL: Yes, my friend, you married an enchanting storybook princess. Such youth at your age is quite damaging. You will go home, find your delinquent wife, and begin again. Forget your lunch pail. Philosophy can only make a man alchoholic.

KEMPLER: If God were only so kind.

COLONEL: God barters.

KEMPLER: God is barbaric.

COLONEL: Only in the movies.

KEMPLER: Do you go to the movies, Colonel?

COLONEL: Yes, on occasion.

KEMPLER: I only like sad movies.

COLONEL: I like the cowboy movies. We all like the cowboy movies, Mister Kempler. You ought to try acting like a cowboy. You can make campfire at night, and kiss your horse sweet dreams. You put me in a strange mood tonight. One more drink for the road?

KEMPLER: Thank you.

COLONEL: *(Pouring drinks)* I like you without your necktie.

KEMPLER: Do you?

COLONEL: But you sit like you have a rifle up your trousers.

KEMPLER: It's the overtime at the drafting table.

COLONEL: Drink up, it might be hard to buy drinks outside.

KEMPLER: To yesterday's happiness.

(COLONEL *and* KEMPLER *drink in unison.*)

KEMPLER: Are you superstitious, Colonel?

COLONEL: No. Are you?

KEMPLER: I fear shadows which dance on the old city walls. Sometimes I notice clear patterns. It's her portrait. Unmistakeable. More and more it occurred to me that Abril is possessed.

COLONEL: Possessed?

KEMPLER: That the Devil has entered her.

COLONEL: You don't believe that.

KEMPLER: No, of course not.

COLONEL: It is a stupid belief.

KEMPLER: Many people believe otherwise.

COLONEL: Surely not you.

KEMPLER: Only the Devil can alter someone.

COLONEL: Please, no ghost stories this evening. Your wife is not possessed. It is out of the question. She is too intelligent to be possessed. *(Pause)* Where is your wife, Mister Kempler?

KEMPLER: I killed her.

COLONEL: Where is your wife?

KEMPLER: You should know.

COLONEL: Where is she, Mister Kempler?

KEMPLER: Hell, for all I care. You needn't act
bewildered.

COLONEL: Why do you persist with this joke?

KEMPLER: Take down my confession, Colonel. I'll make
it easy for you. Friend to friend.

COLONEL: Don't make a fool of me.

KEMPLER: Her body is still warm in the hotel room.

COLONEL: Here in Fez?

KEMPLER: Yes.

COLONEL: Very amusing, Mister Kempler. *(Silence)* You
never told me how you met your wife.

KEMPLER: We met a dozen years ago at a building
project. She represented the banking committee. She
was different then. Very chaste. Very supportive.
Very soft and fragile. I fell for her at once. When I
started courting her I did miraculous things. Expenses
meant nothing to me. We acted like schoolchildren on
holiday. She was so pristine in daylight. So open to my
clumsiness. Patient with my faults. What little faults I
had. Things were simpler then.

COLONEL: As for us all.

KEMPLER: Dear God. Sex alone could not destroy my
wife.

COLONEL: I don't know what does destroy a woman.
Perhaps it is rich living. Perhaps she has taken the
worst your world has provided for her. Perhaps she
is possessed by your Devil. She cannot be taught to be
another way. Not her. That is plain. Devil or no Devil.
(Long pause) How did you murder Mrs Kempler?

KEMPLER: I picked up a clothes iron.

COLONEL: Was death instantaneous?

KEMPLER: I think so.

COLONEL: *(A difficult pause)* Any struggle?

KEMPLER: None.

COLONEL: Look at me, Mister Kempler. *(Pause)* Did you actually have the courage to do it?

KEMPLER: Does it matter? Did she mean anything to you?

COLONEL: As long as you're confessing...

KEMPLER: It was as though I were sleepwalking. I paced the hotel room afterwards looking for loose coins that I had thrown at her. I unwrapped all of the hotel soap, showered vigorously, lunched on the balcony alone, and then dressed to go out.

COLONEL: Why do you patronize me? You don't have the courage to kill a housefly, Mister Kempler. I doubt that you would even raise a hand to your wife.

KEMPLER: I would agree with you, but the truth is...

COLONEL: But the truth is that you are impotent to act.

KEMPLER: Believe what you want.

COLONEL: That is all I can do.

KEMPLER: I am not a coward. I would gladly do it again.

COLONEL: Mister Kempler, your concerns are dear to me. I wish I had medicine for you. This isn't pity. You should have married a Jew as you were no doubt instructed since birth. You would be happier today. Yes, I'm certain of it. I think your blindness is in very poor taste. I don't think you can help yourself either. Do not try to impress me. I pray for you and your wife. If you have done something wrong, do not make me an accomplice.

KEMPLER: I don't need an accomplice.

COLONEL: But you are pointing at me.

KEMPLER: I don't need an accomplice, Colonel. I did everything alone. I stained the bedsheets with her blood and poured her liquid mascara over the head wounds. It was the best that I could do. I couldn't hear her cry. I couldn't explain to her the meaning of her punishment. I couldn't express myself to my wife with more urgency than with a shot to the head. It really was the best that I could do. She sat in the hotel lobby all evening, and there were complaints from the management. I had to carry her upstairs. Yes, she was drunk. Some men were following her. Conversation was impossible. How pathetic we were. I dropped her over the hotel bed. She kicked off her shoes. *(Pause)* And then I killed her.

COLONEL: Must you spoil my evening?

KEMPLER: No, I had no intention of spoiling your evening.

COLONEL: I did not hear any of this.

KEMPLER: There is nothing you did not hear. And there is nothing that you did not see. You can't hurt me anymore.

(MRS KEMPLER *enters, first seen by the* COLONEL *and then* KEMPLER.)

MRS KEMPLER: Charles...

(KEMPLER *reacts.*)

MRS KEMPLER: I want you home. Please come home with me. *(Pause)* Darling...

KEMPLER: Why did you come here?

MRS KEMPLER: I came for you.

KEMPLER: Go. I'll meet you outside.

MRS KEMPLER: Only if you come with me.

KEMPLER: I can't believe your timing.

COLONEL: Go home, Mister Kempler. It's time I closed the office. *(Pause. Awkward)* How nice to see you, Mrs Kempler. Your husband's very entertaining.

MRS KEMPLER: Charles?

COLONEL: He has certain obsessions, Mrs Kempler. Obsessions for storytelling.

MRS KEMPLER: It's an old Semitic tradition... storytelling. How good we all are at it. *(Pause)* Shall I tell a story? In a land bound in tradition, a woman is thrown behind bars. To each man stands a ridiculous claim. It is a tangled story. Is she whore or blessed wife? She loves her husband. Reaches out for him again. A second marriage which restores the first. Grant her wish? Love. Renewal. An everlasting vow. If he reconsiders, Scheherazade is spared another night. Until tomorrow. Until death's blade. Until tomorrow. *(Pause)* Are you content?

KEMPLER: *(Dignified restraint)* Yes.

MRS KEMPLER: *(Pause)* Any further business?

KEMPLER: *(Approaching her)* No further business.

MRS KEMPLER: *(Turning to the* COLONEL*)* Did you say anything wrong to my husband?

(COLONEL *is silent, expressionless.)*

MRS KEMPLER: *Wash kedebti-L-rajali? (Did you say anything wrong to my husband?)*

COLONEL: *La Abadan (No. Never.)*

MRS KEMPLER: *Wakha. Kul shi mezyen. ("Fine. Everything is alright.")*

COLONEL: *Ma Kaynsh sabab. Barakallafikum. ("There would be no reason. God's blessing on you.")* God's blessing on you.

MRS KEMPLER: *(Walking slowly to* KEMPLER *to exit.)* Charles...

*(*KEMPLER *and* MRS KEMPLER *are now arm in arm.)*

COLONEL: *(With off-handed charm)* Do visit us again.

MRS KEMPLER: As far as I'm concerned, we never met.

COLONEL: As you wish.

MRS KEMPLER: *(Lingering moment) Maa-sa-lama. (Goodbye.)*

COLONEL: *(Stirring to best posture) Maa-sa-lama,* Mrs. Kempler. *(After a beat, retrieving envelope of photographs for* KEMPLER, *extending hand)* Mister Kempler...

*(*KEMPLER *makes no effort to receive photos.* COLONEL's *hand drops slowly as lights fade to blackout.)*

END OF PLAY